The Sugar Shack

written by Stacy Snyder • illustrated by Anne Johnson

The Sugar Shack. Ages 3-9.

Text copyright ©2019 by Stacy Snyder. Illustration copyright ©2019 by Anne Johnson.

For information please contact anne@wagdesign.be or stacysnyder@mac.com

Second edition: USA 2020 ISBN: 978-0-9600041-3-3

This book is based on the true story
of two rescue animals who found each other
and became Best Friends.

I was a scruffy mess when I found my friends
Charger and the Lady in the Red Hat.

I had not been bathed or brushed
my entire life.

The Lady in the Red Hat and Charger took me into their yard of beautiful flowers and bathed me, brushed me, and trimmed my mane and tail.

They made me feel loved and accepted.

"We need to find Sugar a place to stay!"
Charger ran to the back yard where an old greenhouse stood.
"Oh my goodness Charger, this is perfect!"

6

They went to work cleaning and painting my new home.

The Lady in the Red Hat found an old couch
and placed it next to the greenhouse.
"We will name your new home the Sugar Shack."

SUGAR SHACK

—As time went by I learned the feeling of being loved.
I was not scared of every sound and movement anymore.
I felt safe.

LIFE WAS GOOD !

One bright sunny morning,

I awoke from a happy dream.

It was about my parents.
I started to wonder
where they might be.

That afternoon, while Charger was visiting me, I asked,
"Will you help me find my parents?"

Charger responded, "I will help but I can't be gone too long.
I don't want the Lady in the Red Hat to worry about me."

"Great! First we will need to find Sticker."

"Who is Sticker?" asked Charger.

I answered,
"Sticker is my friend, a special tree frog.
He knows everything about this area."

11

That morning, Charger opened the gate to the Sugar Shack
and off we went in search of Sticker, the frog.
We ran through fields, crossed rivers, and finally—

came upon a tree, where Sticker was sitting
beneath his friend Henry the Hawk.

When Sticker saw me and Charger
he jumped with joy,
and swam to a lily pad to greet us.

13

"Sticker, I am so happy to see you!
Can you help me find my parents."
Sticker hopped onto my back and joyfully croaked,
"Of course I will help you, and Henry the Hawk can help us too!"

Since it was getting late,
Charger needed to get back
to the Lady in the Red Hat,
so she said her goodbyes—
and went on her way.

The next day,

Henry flew high in the clear blue sky.

Then, with a loud ribbit, Sticker cried,

"Henry, flying up so high—
Tell us what you see.
Guide us from the sky—
To set Sugar's parents free."

After circling above the treetops
Henry landed in a tree to rest.
There below sat a crow.

"Who are you?" asked Henry.

"I am Cranky the Crow.
Why do you fly around in circles?"

Henry responded,
"I am looking for Sugar's parents."

Cranky squawked, "You will never find them."

Henry proudly replied,
"Well, when I think good thoughts— good things happen."

That day, Henry soared through the sky. Suddenly, Cranky made a loud skreech.

Oh no! Now what? thought Henry. But this time, Cranky had something nice to say.

"Skree.. ...eeetch!"

"Henry, I took your advice to think good thoughts and guess what?"

"I realized I have three new friends which makes me happy! I hope you find Sugar's parents and maybe my positive thoughts will help too."

19

That night I looked up at the Moon and Sparkle,

"Oh Moon and Sparkle shining bright
I'm asking for your help tonight—
The loss of my parents is so bad.
Help me find them, I am so sad."

The Moon replied with a smile,

"Tomorrow my position flips—
There will be a solar eclipse.
In the darkness of the hour
I will be at fullest power—
I promise all will be made anew,
Your Mom and Dad will be shown to you."

21

We walked on while Henry flew close above.
We followed the Moon's path, protecting our eyes
from the bright white light of the eclipse—

and as the Sun came out of the Moon's shadow
they found themselves in front of an old shed.

Not knowing what to expect,
I looked inside, and much to my surprise,
there lay my parents.

They looked old and tired
from years of dancing and prancing.

My parents whinnied with excitement
and their faces lit up with happiness.

I whinnied,
"Mom and Dad I have missed you.
Let me take you home to the Sugar Shack.

My parents were overwhelmed
with joy to be with me.

That afternoon,
we planned our journey back to the Sugar Shack.

Here we go!

Discover the journey back in the next book,

Sugar's Journey Home.

Now go back and see if you can spot any of these friendly little creatures.

Hummingbird

Lamb

Black Spider

Red Robin

Raccoon

Grasshopper

Snail

Hedgehog

Turtle

STACY SNYDER is a graduate of the University of Arizona, with a degree in Special Education. She resides in San Diego California, with her loving husband John. She is the mother of two daughters, and the grandmother of four beautiful grandchildren. Her background in education and love for nature were the inspiration for this book. She was taken by the extraordinary relationship that developed between a rescued dog and a rescued miniature horse. Their unconditional love is a heart-warming example of kindness.

ANNE JOHNSON has held a career in painting, illustration and fine arts for over 30 years. She received a Bachelor of Arts degree from Roanoke College followed by a Master of Arts degree in Medical Illustration from the Medical College of Georgia. She has an endless love for animals and nature and has been passionate about children's books since she was a young girl. Born and raised in Minnesota, she currently resides in Belgium and is the proud mother of three loving young adults, two dogs, a cat, and a horse. *The Sugar Shack* is her second book with Stacy Snyder.

SUGAR is a rescued buckskin miniature horse. She was in very poor shape when she was adopted. Scared and very skittish. With patience and spending lots of time with her, she has become a loving, contented horse with the help of her friend Charger. Age unknown.

CHARGER was adopted as a puppy, and has grown into a large, strong dog with a very happy disposition. Charger loves to go on walks with her best friend Sugar on a double leash. She also insists on wearing sunglasses. Charger is 10 years old.

This sequel is dedicated to
the beautiful children, grand-children, cousins, nieces and nephews
that have all played an important part in its development.

Thanks to the loving support of this close-knit family
and the special bond between the author and the artist,
this book series is able to continue.

We would like to give special thanks to
the wonderful librarians of the Rancho Santa Fe Library
for their invaluable time, meticulous input and endless support.

Use these blank pages to draw any of your favorite characters.

www.ingramcontent.com/pod-product-compliance
Lightning Source LLC
Chambersburg PA
CBHW040404100426

42811CB00017B/1835

* 9 7 8 0 9 6 0 0 0 4 1 3 3 *